Socialism

The Socialist Party of Great Britain

Contents

PREFACE TO THIRD EDITION

THE first edition of this pamphlet, which amounted to 20,000 copies, was sold out some time ago. The delay in bringing out the second edition has been due to that bugbear of working-class organisations— lack of funds. Perhaps those who are interested in seeing more pamphlets produced by us and who are able to spare a little towards this end, will bear that fact in mind. The more funds we have the more literature we will produce.

In bringing out this second edition we have brought some of the illustrations up to date and deleted others that are too old to be interesting and illuminating. We have also revised the text in places where we thought greater clearness of presentation would be achieved by so doing.

Our aim has been to give our fellow-workers as clear and concise a picture of their present position in society as is possible in a pamphlet of this size. How far we have succeeded is for the reader to judge.

At a time when attempts are being made, in various parts of the world, to crush out all working-class aspirations and to convert the worker into a dumb and placid beast of burden, it is imperative that workers, wherever possible, should understand why they are poor and how to end their poverty. The explanation and the answer are given in the following pages. We urge the reader to give them his careful and unbiased consideration.

August, 1933.

Reprinted May, 1941

Who are the Working Class?

These words are addressed to the members of the working class. Let us, then, explain whom we mean when we speak of the working class.

In political economy a class is a body of people united by what are called economic interests, or, to put it another way, material interests, or wealth interests, or bread-and-butter interests—the interest, makes the class.

The economic or wealth interests of a class, though they may clash as far as individuals are concerned, are, as against the interests of another class, a united and solid whole.

We do not intend, at this early stage, to go into the matter of what causes the division of society into classes. It is sufficient for the present to say that society to-day is divided into classes —into two. classes, one of which is. called the working class, because its members have to work for their living, and the other of which is called the capitalist class because those who compose it, owning the land, mines, factories, machinery, railways, raw material and. the like, use them for the purpose of making a profit.

Now the line between.- those who have to work and. those who do not is not sufficiently clear for us to explain by it the class position of every individual—neither is the line between those who possess and those who do not possess. Many capitalists work in some capacity or other without becoming thereby members of the working class,. while many a working man has a share or two in some industrial concern, but this does not make him a capitalist.

Nevertheless, the fact of possession or non-possession at bottom determines which class a man belongs to, and sets up those distinctions by which we shall show who are the members of the working class.

Since people can only live on the wealth which is produced, and since all the means of producing that, wealth (the land, mines, factories, machinery, and so on) are in the possession of some of the people to the exclusion of the others, it is clear that those who possess and those who do not possess are placed in very different circumstances.

Those who possess have in their hands the means of living, and more than this, they are able to deny to those who do not possess all I access to the means of life.. To draw upon our common knowledge, the only terms upon which the non-possessors are allowed access to the means of living are that the)- must become the employees of the owners. In other words, they must sell to the owners their mental and physical energies, the working power which is contained within their bodies.

This is the distinction which marks off the member of the working class from the capitalist. The former is compelled to sell his bodily powers in order to live. In comparison what else matters? What does it matter whether these bodily powers are skilled or unskilled or whether that for which they are sold is called wages or salary? What does it matter whether the labour upon which those bodily powers are expended is performed with a pen or a pickaxe, or in an office, a workshop, a factory, a mine, or the street? What does it matter whether the worker is well paid or ill paid, or whether he is a professional, clerical or so-called manual worker?

The essential thing is that the member of the working class has to sell his labour-power in order to live. Beside this salient fact all else pales into insignificance. The differences of dress, pay, education, habits, work, -and so on that, are to be observed among those who have to sell their working power in order to live are as nothing compared with the differences which mark, them off from capitalists No matter how well paid the former is, or how many have. to obey his commands, he himself has a master. He has to render obedience to another, to someone who can-send him adrift to endure the torments of unemployment. Because he has to sell his labour-power his whole life must be lived within prescribed limits. His release from the need to labour is short and seldom; he has no security of livelihood; he has always to fear that a rival may displace him.

On the other hand, the capitalist, because he is able to deny others access to the means of living, and is. therefore, able to compel them to surrender their labour-power to him, is relieved from the necessity of working. His conditions of life are essentially different from those of the worker—different, not in one or two particulars, but in practically every particular. Ease and luxury are only the most obvious features of a life which has little in common with that of the working class.

For him are leisure and freedom—for the others the fetters of constant toil; for him are the Riviera, and the Alps—for the others, the office prison, the weary workshop, the choking town, or the drab country labour yard. And yet the complete story cannot be told in these inadequate comparisons. The whole world is the capitalist's, and-the workers live their hard round simply to enable the capitalist to enjoy his world.

These words, then are addressed to all those who in order to live, have to sell their labour-power, whether "mental" or "manual" "skilled" or "unskilled," high-paid or low-paid, for wages or salary.

Why all Workers Should Read this Pamphlet

Those who address these pages to the reader are working-class men and women—clerks and taxi-men, artists and accountants, shopmen and sweeps, carpenters, " bricklayers, masons, excavators, plumbers, painters, journalists, printers, scientific workers, weavers, porters, and men of many other trades—but all working-class people; all folk who depend for their livelihood on the sale of their own labour-power, or the sale of the labour-power of those who are their breadwinners.

The men and women, then, who address you through these pages are in die same position as you are. They work side by side with you in the office, workshop or factory; they face death and disablement with you in the mine; they "fight shoulder to shoulder with "you in the strike; they know what it is to walk the streets day after day in vain search for employment. The experience of poverty and humiliation which has seared your minds has Burnt also into theirs.

We ask your earnest consideration of the pages that follow, because, being of the same class, suffering the same ills that you suffer we know that only with your deliverance can we be delivered.

The means of production and distribution which you, made and which you renew and enlarge belong to the capitalists. The wealth which you produce provides, for the whole race. Yet only part of it goes to the working class, who produce it, while the rest goes to the master class, who do not. It is plain that the more the' masters take, the less there is for you, and the, more you secure the less there remains for the masters.

What does this mean? Can it mean anything else than opposing interests? Of course it cannot. It is the interest of each class to obtain more of the wealth produced, and since the more either class gets the less there is left for the other, their interests must clash.

The capitalists admit that the more they get of the wealth produced the less is left for the workers, but they deny that there are opposing interests. They claim that the interest of both classes is to combine to produce more wealth. We shall show presently that to produce more wealth by no means necessarily increases either the absolute or the relative portion received by the producers; But even if it were true .that the interest of both classes is to combine to produce more wealth, it ;would remain as true as ever that it would be to the interest of each to obtain the largest possible share, of the "wealth produced, and hence the class interests would still clash.

As a matter of fact, the classes do combine, willingly or unwillingly, but very effectually, to produce ever greater wealth, yet although they succeed in this, the signs of opposing interests, strikes and lock-outs, remain as glaring as ever.

It is because it is so plainly the interest of the capitalist class to do all they can to prevent the workers obtaining ownership and control of the means of production and distribution: and more of the wealth they produce, and, therefore, above all, to keep them from learning why they are poor, and how to throw off their poverty, that the latter must look only to their own class for help. They must examine closely every message that is opposed and reviled by the masters and by their instruments and hirelings— their press, parsons, and politicians.

It is for these reasons that all workers should read this pamphlet

Is There Wealth Enough?

We workers are not in a position to undertake elaborate scientific researches for ourselves. We have to base our conclusions largely on the work of the experts employed by the capitalist class. This, however, relieves the statistics from all suspicion of bias in our own favour.

When we say that the poverty and hardship which exists among the working class of every country to-day is unnecessary, defenders of capitalism tell us that we -are wrong. They tell us that there always have been poor people, and that, therefore,, there always must be. They tell us, further that although, some people are very men, there really is not sufficient wealth produced _ to abolish poverty even if it were equally distributed.

The absurdity of this, however, is easily shown. The late Sir Henry Campbell-Bannerman, who, was Prime Minister. from 1905 to 1908, speaking at Perth in June, 1903 said: "In this country we know, thanks to the patience and accurate scientific, investigations of Mr. Rowntree and Mr. Charles Booths that there is about 30 per cent, of our population underfed, on the verge of hunger, about 30 per cent, of the population is living in the grip of perpetual poverty ..."

The term " poverty" is, of course, a relative one. But Sir H. Campbell-Bannerman had something very definite in his mind when he said " about 30 per cent, of the population is living in the grip of perpetual poverty.

He quoted-Mr. Rowntree and Mr, Charles Booth as his authorities.

Mr. Rowntree carried out his investigations in York, a typical provincial city. For the purpose of providing a feasts for his statistics, he drew an imaginary poverty line, which he calculated would provide the primary necessaries for a family of five persons, at lowest co-operative store prices. " Here is Mr. Rowntree's " Primary Poverty Line " :

Food. 12 shillings 9d

Rent and Rates 4 shillings

Clothing, including Boots 2 shillings 3d

Fuel 1 shilling 10d

Lighting, washing materials, furniture, crockery, etc. 10d

Total 21 shillings 8d

The dietary in this estimate was so stringent that no butcher's meat is allowed, and tea but once a week, while nothing is reckoned for drink and. tobacco. Newspapers are not provided for, nor postage, nor bus, tram or railway fares, nor theatres;, nor any form "of recreation, while medicines, medical attendance, insurance, and all the amenities of our boasted civilisation, have to be paid for with what is left out of 10d. a week, after lighting, washing materials, furniture, and crockery have been purchased for a family of five!

It cannot be said that this extreme poverty of nearly one-third of the population was caused by the smallness of the amount of wealth produced at that time, -and that the poverty was consequently unavoidable. On the contrary, while these workers were deprived even of necessities, there were many wealthy persons receiving incomes far in excess of reasonable needs. Sir Leo Chiozza Money, then a Liberal M.P., estimated in 1904 that one-third of the entire income of this country was being enjoyed by a small body of people numbering less than one-thirtieth of-the population (see " Riches and Poverty" p. 42). He said that if the national income had been divided equally among the whole population each family of five persons would have received about £200 a year, i.e., about 77s. a week. Yet there were these thousands of families trying to live on 21s. 8d. or less.

We have taken for our illustration the condition of affairs in 1903 eleven years1 before the Great War. The choice of date is deliberate, It is a final answer to those people who have tried to accuse the poverty which still exists on the ground that it is the result of the War.

If we take a more recent investigation into the extent of the extreme poverty measured by Rowntree and others, we find that there has indeed been, some improvement in the position of the poorest section of the workers. According to the "New Survey of London Life and Labour," the amount of extreme poverty in the East End of London has declined somewhat since 1890,' when Charles Booth made his investigation. Nevertheless, over 19 per cent, of families (one family in every five) in Stepney and Poplar were in poverty in 1929 (p. 80). :By " poverty " the investigator meant a standard which allows only 39s. for a family of man, wife and two children, aged 10 and 4. (p. 74). it is important to remember, too that when this investigation was being made unemployment was not much more than 1,000,000. In 1931-1933 it had increased to between. "2.5 and 3 millions—with an inevitable increase in the percentage of persons below the "poverty line"

Although there has "been some improvement in the position of the poorest workers (accompanied by a worsening in the position of many groups who formerly were somewhat better off) the inequality between the rich, and the poor is as great as, if not greater than, before the War.

It is still true that a small minority of the population receives a disproportionate share of the wealth. For example Lord Arnold, Paymaster-General in" the Labour Government, stated in 1931 that there were at the time probably 90,000 super-tax payers who, after all their taxes had been paid, were enjoying an average income of about £60 a week each. (Daily Herald, 13th April, 1931)

Even with the present wasteful use "of the productive forces there is enough wealth produced to raise the standard of living of the great mass of the population. Mr. Colin Clark, M.A., in his recent book, "The National Income, 1924-1931" (published in 1932 by MacMillan & Co., Ltd.), estimates that if the total national income were equally distributed, every family would have received about £349 during 1929, £341 during 1930 and £298 during 1931 (see p. 78). These, amounts are equal to about £6 14s 0d a week, £6 11s 0d a week and £5 15s 0d a week for the years in question.

These figures may be compared with the earnings of male workers employed in a number of industries in October 1931, based on an inquiry made by the Ministry of Labour (see Labour Gazette, January, 1933) According to this inquiry the average weekly earnings of male workers employed in large firms employing ten or more ranged from 36s. 8d. in the linen industry and 41s. in the jute industry up to 60s. Id. in silk and artificial silk and 72s. 7d, in the fur trade. The average earnings of cotton workers were 45s; 3d. a week, of ready-made boot and shoemakers 52s, 10d., of workers in motor engineering 61s. 8d. (larger firms) and 47s 8d_. (smaller firms). The above figures relate to male workers of all ages. If the workers without families were excluded the average- earnings would, of course, be somewhat higher, but even after making all due allowance for this, the difference between the workers' actual pay and the amount which would result from the equal distribution referred to by Mr. Clark is obviously very considerable.

The great inequality of income is, moreover, only one aspect of the poverty problem. Capitalism not only bestows on the rich a large share of the wealth produced, but-—even more important —it keeps the amount of wealth produced far below the possible total. . Various aspects of this evil effect of the capitalist social system are explained in the section which follows.

The Possibility of Leisure

And now with regard to leisure; think what an enormous margin of labour power exists today.

In the first place, the Statistical Memoranda (Cd. 4671), published by the Local Government Board, tell us that the " percentage of members of Trade Unions making returns who were out of employment, not including members on strike, on sick pay, of on superannuation benefit," in the year 1904, when the amount of wealth mentioned by Sir Leo Money was produced, was 6 8.

It is generally admitted that these returns understate the full extent of unemployment; but if we accept them as indicative of the whole, we had among the 15 million workers of the country about a million in enforced idleness.

After the war the army of unemployed reached 2-millions in 1921, then after fluctuating for some years between 1 and 1 millions, grew rapidly in 1930 and 1931 until it was in the region of 3 millions. Even the most optimistic defender of capitalism does not expect it to fall below 1 million again.

The 5 million persons belonging to the master class produce nothing. If these contributed workers in the same ratio as the rest of the population, there would be another 2,000,000 workers available for production.

The numbers of men removed from useful labour by the coercive forces are roughly: the army, 200,000; the navy and air force, 130,000; police and prison staffs, 70,000; while there are nearly 80,000 persons employed by the Churches and other religious bodies chasing the shadow instead of wrestling with the substance.

These groups of people frittering away their energies either from choice or compulsion, total over 2\ millions in addition to the unemployed.

But this is not all. According to the census returns for 1921, 81,347 commercial travellers were scouring the country in England and Wales alone, with no better object than to snatch trade from rivals; and 539,686 male and 426,475 female clerks and typists were' toiling, to a great extent uselessly, in stuffy business offices. The streets teem with canvassers and agents and door-to-door distributors. Bakers' carts chase each other over the same ground; butchers' carts and milk carts do the same. Myriads of petty shopkeepers wait at a myriad counters for customers who do not come. The great increase in the numbers employed in the distributive trades (an addition of 700,000 between 1923 and 1932) to a large extent represents labour transferred from the productive trades.

Over 1.5 million persons (excluding clerks) are employed in commerce, finance and insurance.

The millions who neither toil nor spin are waited upon by thousands upon thousands of servants and flunkeys, who add nothing to the national wealth. . The railways call for numerous booking clerks to serve out tickets, and collectors to punch them and collect them. The 'buses and trams are overrun with spying inspectors.

The number of people in England and Wales engaged in 1921 in the building and allied trades; mining and quarrying; metal, engineering and shipbuilding; textile, tailoring, boot and shoe trades3 food, drink and tobacco; electrical apparatus making and fitting, etc.; wood and furniture trades; and agriculture, was only 7,615;198—and these figures included all persons over 12, and employers as well as the unemployed in those industries.

Nearly the whole of the wealth of the country is produced by the workers engaged in these trades, whose numbers equalled about half the male population of the country between the ages of 16 and 60, at the time the figures were taken. So, after balancing the wealth producers in other trades, and those engaged in transport, against the unemployed and employers in these, it is reasonable to claim that the whole of the nation's "wealth can be produced by the male population between 16 and 60 years of age working half the time they do now.

Another striking illustration of the productive powers of the working class is offered by the experience of the war. In 1917 and 1918 no less than four million fit men were in the forces. Only 1,600,000 additional women workers were employed in industry, yet it was possible to maintain the supply of. essential goods and services, and at the same time produce in colossal quantities the weapons of destruction for British and AUfed armies. As Sir Leo Chiozza Money said; our "productive powers actually increased ' ("Triumph of Nationalisation," page 137.)

In order, then, that plenty and leisure may be the portion of all, we need not wait for further advances in the means of production. Every requisite is already in the hands of society, and it only remains for human intelligence so to organise the existing powers of production, and so to arrange the distribution of wealth already being produced, as to make the best use of both. Then poverty and drudgery will be banished for ever.

The human intelligence which accomplishes this, since it can do it only by dislodging the rich from their position of idle luxury and privilege, must necessarily come from the working class.

The Cause of Poverty

Let us now enquire how poverty arises in this " age of plenty as a preliminary to considering how it may be abolished

It may not be amiss here to remind the reader again how obviously wrong are those people who ascribe the poverty and unemployment of the workers to the war.

Mr. Rowntree says that in a year of good trade, before the war. 15 per cent, of the working class, or 10 per cent, of the whole population of York, were living actually below the poverty line, while 28 per cent, of the entire population of that city were living below, upon, or very little above it.

Mr. Charles Booth concluded from his researches in London that 30.7 per cent, of the population (or assuming the national ratio of workers to capitalist about 36 per cent, of the working-class population) of the metropolis were living in similar conditions of poverty, and other investigators working in ether cities have arrived at identical results.

This, mark you, was the state of things in a " year of good trade" with unemployment at a low level. Hence, unemployment had not a great deal to do with it. Obviously, if unemployment had been the cause of poverty it would need much more than 6.8 per cent, of unemployment to explain the terrible plight of 36 per cent, of the whole working class.

Unemployment is not the cause of poverty. The workers are poor while they are earning wages. They are poor because their wages are insufficient.

We have first, then, to discover how wages are determined.

How Wages are Determined

Wages are the price of something that is sold. The prices of all other things rise and fall with the changing relations of supply and demand. So also with wages.

But these changes only cause wages to fluctuate about a certain point—they do. not determine that point. In fact, they cannot determine that any more than the finger which plucks a banjo string determines the line about which the string vibrates. What, then, does determine the point about which wages vary. Why, when supply and demand equal each other, do wages not find a higher or lower level?

What, first of all, is it that the worker sells? It is not actual labour, – for that does not exist at the time of the sale. It is labour-power.

Labour-power and labour are two different things. Labour-power is contained within the worker's body, and so belongs to him, and can be sold by him. It only becomes labour by being put out from his body—by the process of working. When he has converted his labour-power into labour, the labourer's power has ceased to exist. It has been turned into something else. He has, in very fact and deed, "put out his strength "—turned it into labour, which is now resident, not in himself, but in the material upon which he has been working.

It is quite evident from this that the wage-labourer cannot sell his labour, for as soon as it is performed, it is contained with in the material belongings to his employer, and it, therefore, belongs to his employer, the owner of the substance in which it is embodied. The labour is sold in the form of finished products, for the benefit of the employer.

The worker, then, sells his labour-power for wages,, and. wages, we have seen fluctuate with supply and demand.

We were asking what determines the point about which this fluctuation takes place. It cannot be supply and demand, for they only determine the vibration; they are the finger that plucks the string. We want the equivalent of the bridge and nut which support the string.

A sale is an exchange of one object for another, and what we are asking for is the standard by which labour-power is measured against money.

Different things are measured against one another by the qualities they possess in common. Thus bread may be measured on the scales by means of an iron weight, because, and only because, both the bread and the iron possess one quality in common—weight. And when you have balanced them, you know that they each possess the same quantity of the quality, weight, and, therefore, they are equals in that respect. All you have done, in fact, by weighing them is to declare that, no matter how they may differ in bulk,, texture, colour, or other quality, they are equals in weight.

Similarly, you may measure out a pint of peas and a pint of beer in a pint pot, and declare them equal bulks, but you can only do this because they both possess bulk.

But all things of value can be measured against gold, no matter how diverse may be' their character. A ton of coal and a quarter of an ounce of gold, we may say, are worth each other. They are equals, but in what respect? We have only five senses, and all the physical qualities of the gold and the coal must make themselves known through those senses or remain unknown. Are they the same to the touch, taste, sight, smell, or hearing?

No, they are not.

Their equality cannot be due to their utility, for the things which are useful to the largest number of people are the cheapest. The race cannot exist without food, but could get along very well without gold-—much better than without iron; yet of how much greater worth is gold (in exchange) than an equal weight either of bread or iron!

If a ton of coal is worth, say, £2 in London, we know that at the pit mouth it will be worth only about half that amount. Whatever quality the coal and gold possess in common, and by means of which they are compared, as values, is possessed by them in different proportions at, say, Newcastle and London. Yet both possess exactly the same physical properties and-the same utility in both places.

The only way in which coal in Newcastle differs from coal in London is in the amount of labour which it has absorbed; this, then, must be. the common quality by means" of which the coal and gold are measured.

It is so in fact—but with certain qualifications. The labour must be necessary labour. Carrying coal to London is necessary labour,- because coal is needed there, and there are no mines in the vicinity. Carrying the coal to London by rail or boat is necessary labour because they are the most economical means; but carrying it by pack-horse would not be necessary labour, because much less wasteful means are available.

Labour, then, is the common quality possessed by all things of value, and by which they are measured. To say, therefore, that two tons of coal are worth £2 at Newcastle is simply to say that it has taken the same amount or necessary labour to produce the coal as it has taken to produce the gold. In London about one ton would contain the labour equal to that contained in the £2.

One of the things that regularly exchange for gold is labour-power. Labour-power has no quality in common with gold except the labour that is embodied in it. The labour which is embodied in labour-power is the labour contained in the food, clothing, shelter, etc., consumed by the worker, in producing his labour-power. Thus the necessary labour involved in producing labour-power is fro more and no less than that contained in the worker's means of subsistence.

We have now got that equivalent to the bridge and nut which support the vibrating string, that something which determines the point about which supply and demand shall cause wages to fluctuate. It is the cost of subsistence.

Let us now summarise our conclusions.

(1) The price of all exchangeable things fluctuates with the changing ratio of supply to demand

(2) The point about which the price fluctuates is not determined by supply and demand, but by value.

(3) This value 'is not altered by supply and demand, though the price is, therefore price and value do not always correspond—things sell at onetime above and at another below their value.

(4) Nevertheless, since value determines the point about which price fluctuates, when these fluctuations cancel one another an average is struck which corresponds to value; therefore the average of price or prices, in the long run are identical with value1

(5) Value is determined by the amount of necessary labour required to produce the exchangeable thing at the time and

place at which it is required. It follows, then, that prices in the long run are determined by the cost in labour {not the cost of labour, i.e., wages, which have nothing to do with it, but the cost in hours of labour) necessary to the production of the goods or commodities.

Now to apply these conclusions to labour-power and wages.

(a) Wages, being the price of labour-power, fluctuate under the influence of supply and demand.

(b) The point about which wages fluctuate is determined by the value of labour-power.

(c) The value of labour-power depends on the amount of labour-necessary to produce it. That labour is the labour embodied in the wealth which forms the subsistence of the worker and his dependents; therefore,

(d) Wages are determined, in -the long run, by the cost of the workers' subsistence.

Two things help to bring about this result. First, given the present Standard of subsistence, wages cannot for any extended time fail below the cost of this standard, or the labour-power cannot be produced; secondly, wages cannot for long rise above this point because there is always an army of unemployed whose competition for work keeps wages down.

The reader is invited to turn again to Mr. Rowntree's terrible " Poverty Line," of 21s; 8d., on or below which he and' others found, by "accurate and scientific investigation," nearly a third of the population of this country was living, or to the recent survey in the East End of London, and to consider how correctly our deductions are drawn from facts. Our conclusions point to the finding that the workers, as a class, get no more than enough to reproduce the standard of efficiency required by the employers.

The Cause of Unemployment

It is seen that the general insufficiency of wages to lift the workers above poverty is due to the operation of economic forces which determine that wages shall approximate to the' subsistence level. We will now turn to unemployment.

There are two aspects—the constant and the periodic. We will deal with the constant first.

When an employer buys labour-power he buys it in order to produce wealth. But his. object is not simply to produce wealth. The law of the land demands that he shall, in view of the possibility that the official receiver in bankruptcy may at any time develop an unwelcome interest in his affairs, keep certain books recording his transactions.

Any worker who has to keep those books for his employer knows that each of those records starts with money—the money thrown into the process in which the concern is engaged —and ends with money—the money that comes back with the sale of the product. Indeed, this is hardly correct, for the record, strictly speaking, is not complete until a balance has been struck showing the difference between the two sums. The process is not, therefore, one of producing goods and selling them in- order to produce more goods, but one of putting money into production in order to get money.

But the essence of the transaction is not simply the turning of money into money. To spend £1 in labour-power wherewith to produce wealth which- one sells for £1 is only exchanging one £1 note for another, which is absurd. To record only such transactions would soon bring even the wealthiest firms into troubled waters. The money realised at the end of the transaction must differ from that spent at the beginning. It can only, in the eye of the book-keeper, differ in amount—it must be greater. Therefore, it is this difference, this increase, or surplus, alone which impels the capitalist to engage in production.

The purchaser of labour-power, therefore, endeavours to make that surplus as large as he possibly can.

Now, there are several ways of doing this. He may cut down wages, he may lengthen the working hours, he may introduce new methods and organisation. But the most important means he has at hand for increasing the surplus wealth is machinery.

New mechanical devices for rendering labour-power more productive are always being developed and constantly being adopted. This unceasing introduction of machinery has the effect of continually reducing the number of people required to produce a given amount of wealth. Every advance of machinery at the same time makes greater the difference between what the worker produces and what he buys back (because his product increases while his wages remain relatively stationary). The result is that production increases more rapidly than demand in the established trades, and consequently the workers find their labour-power unsaleable. In this way improved machinery and methods increase the insecurity of even most highly trained workers who were accustomed to consider their occupations permanent. Even if they find employment in the new industries, their condition is likely to be worse than before.

Now for the second aspect of the same process, in (their anxiety to obtain a .surplus, the employers, when the markets are favourable, strain every nerve and fibre to increase their output. New machinery is laid down; fresh 'hands' are taken on; overtime is worked. There is an expansion of trade such as occurred in the years up to 1929. Then, at the very height of the expansion, reaction sets in.

Production in certain industries has outstripped demand; the markets are glutted and the warehouses full to bursting. Orders have fallen oft and products have become unsaleable. Workers are discharged, and these, losing their purchasing power with the loss of their wages, affect other industries, and so the depression spreads. Soon there is a crisis and the Labour Exchanges are thronged with unemployed—a crisis and semi-starvation—not because of sterility or famine, but because of the productiveness of human labour; not because the necessaries of life are scarce, but because they are too abundant!

The existence of unemployment, as regards its constant aspect, is seen to arise from the development of the means of production under private ownership, and with regard to its aspect of periodic severity, from unrestrained output in the wild scramble of the capitalists for the surplus which results from the exploitation of the wage-workers.

Can unemployment be removed by shortening the hours of labour? And can poverty be abolished by higher wages? Machinery and organisation prevent these proposals from being permanently effective.

The Effects of Machine Development

It may be stated as a preliminary that every increase in the price of labour-power tends to hasten the development of machinery. Many people do not grasp this because they fail to understand the general condition of the instruments of labour. They mink that, for the statement to be correct, every increase in the price of labour-power must give birth to a number of new inventions, and they say inventions are not made to order.

This, however, is a wrong view to take. In almost every industry the instruments of labour vary very much as regards their stage of development. Thus, in the printing of posters, some firms who print enormous numbers do them on special machines, others lower in the scale print them on the general purposes machine, while yet others can employ nothing better than a hand press. But there are degrees among presses, and while many posters are run off

on modern presses, here and there the " Stanhope " of our great-grandfathers clanks its tardy way to destruction.

Every industry may be viewed as a sort of inclined plane down which machines are more or less steadily slipping to the scrap heap. No matter how useful a machine may be, it is not profitable or advantageous to every firm in the industry. Above are those to whom it is not sufficiently economical, below are those who find it beyond their reach. .

But always, both above and below, there is a fringe of doubt, on the one hand where users are hesitating whether to relinquish it for something higher in the scale, on the other hand where capitalists are wondering whether it would be sound policy to adopt the machine.

Let us take the Linotype compositing machine for example. This wonderful appliance, though a great labour-saver. Is profitable only to a certain circle of printers— those who have a considerable amount of book or newspaper work. But many are considering the pros and cons of its adoption. A very little will decide. An extra monthly magazine—or perhaps putting in a machine, by saving two or three men's room, will avoid an expensive removal to larger premises.

Now, suppose wages rise, immediately the doubters are decided, They adopt the machine, and each machine throws three or four compositors into the street. Machinery takes a step forward, not by a new invention, but by the wider adoption of what is already invented and in use.

It is quite true that this development of production is always going on, and would continue to some extent in the face even of declining wages. But nevertheless, since machinery is at all times the competitor of the worker, an increase in the cost of labour-power, whether by a direct rise in wages, or by a reduction of working hours or restriction of output, is in the competition between labour-power and machinery, a handicap on labour-power. Desirable as it undoubtedly is, it gives a jolt to the inclined plane, quickens the development of machinery, reduces the number of workers needed to meet the demands of the markets existing at the time, and by forming new armies of out-of works, defeats every attempt to solve the unemployed " problem."

It may be argued that at all events higher wages would have been secured, but it is evident that the higher rates of wages would be subjected to increased pressure from the competition of the new unemployed army.

It is not denied, of course, that legal enactment may, to some extent, prevent fearfully low wages being paid in the so-called sweated industries, but the fact must not be lost sight of that many of these unhappy workers are deprived by such legislation of the opportunity of selling their labour-power at any price. The many earning a pittance by toiling in their own slum dens are enabled to compete with factory machinery and factory organisation only by debasing their standard of living to a point that now and again shocks humanity. But to try to raise their remuneration by minimum wage acts has the effect of making it more to the advantage of the " sweater "to have the work done by a higher type of labour and higher means of production in factories—the effects of the development of machinery again.

That this is some improvement is possible, but as a cure for poverty it fails.

The Struggle for Higher Wages Necessary

It might appear that the condition of the workers is fixed, and that it is useless for them to struggle for better conditions under the present system. The idea is foolish. To say that supply and demand is the immediate regulator of wages is to say that wages find their natural base through competition.. Competition is strife, therefore the operation of the laws of wages presupposes struggle.

In the world of commodities prices in the long run are just as much pre-determined, yet although the fluctuations of price cancel one another and leave an average corresponding to value, buyers and sellers do not cease to struggle over prices.

The exchange of goods at their value is the result of the struggle, and in the same way, the result of the struggle between masters and men is that wages are determined by the cost of subsistence.

The Standard of Comfort

It is not to be supposed, however, that this cost of subsistence is necessarily the very lowest amount of food, clothing, and shelter upon which a man can produce a given amount of energy.

If wages tend to sink to the. level of subsistence, it is to the level of subsistence under the prevailing standard of comfort. We shall see, however, that this does not weaken in the slightest degree the contention that the cost of producing labour-power determines its price.

When the present system arose in England it found a producing class who had emancipated themselves from serfdom and became peasant-proprietors, owning all they produced. They, therefore, were accustomed to a comparatively high standard of living. Fighting on this basis, the working class of this country have maintained a higher standard of comfort than workers elsewhere overtaken by capitalism while they yet had a lower standard of subsistence.

In America, where, instead of a constant drift from the country to the towns, large numbers constantly drifted from the towns to the country, labour-power was very scarce in industrial centres, and a very high standard of subsistence became established in consequence. But, just as in England, the-development of capitalism, and particularly the increasing difficulty of making a living on the land, has resulted in a lowering of the worker's standard. In fifteen chief American industries it has been declining since 1896, between 1896 and 1907 by 6 per cent, and over the whole 24 years to 1920 by nearly 25 per cent. (American Economic Review, September,

1921.)

Some improvement took place between 1921 and 1929, when production was expanding, but most of this gain was lost in the depression which began in 1929. In America, as in England, the capitalists gained most from the increased wealth production during the period of expansion.

Now, how does the law work out to the result that, though there is such a divergence in the standard of living of the respective peoples, that standard everywhere represents the physical limit of exploitation in the given circumstances?

The answer is simple enough. Labour-power, having for its competitor machinery, becomes more intensely exploited where it is dearer, in accordance with the law which provides that as the price of labour-power increases, more and higher grades of machinery are introduced.

This explains why it is that machinery has reached such a high state of development in America compared with what it has in this country, It is not that the inventive faculties of Uncle Sam's children are greater than those of other people. Labour-power, being dearer, provides the condition under which machinery develops most rapidly, that is all. In Victorian England much machinery was designed and manufactured solely for use in America, for the simple reason that labour-power was too cheap to provide an opening for it here.

Many years ago this contrast existed between England and the Continental countries. This is shown by the report of Mr. Commissioner Wells, the Special Commissioner of Revenue in the United States, to Congress in 1868 and the report of Mr. Redgrave, one of the Inspectors of factories. – The former said ("Work and Wages" Brassey, Page 103, First Edition):

Whereas female labour in the cotton manufacture is paid at from 12s to 15s. a week in Great Britain; at from 7s. 3d. to 9s. 7d. in France, Belgium and Germany; at from 2s 4d. to 2s 11d. In Russia: the one thing which is most dreaded by the continental manufacturers everywhere is British competition.

Mr. Redgrave reported (Ibid Page 101)

The average number of persons employed to spindles is—in France, one person to 14 spindles; in Russia one to 28 spindles; in Prussia one to 37; in Great Britain one to 74.

(The explanation of the seeming discrepancy in the case of France compared with Russia is that the French Spindles produced higher quality goods.)

Mr. Thomas Brassey, son of one of the largest contractors of the 19th century, gives in his book, "Work and Wages," many striking instances of the truth of our contention. He says, for example (Pages 67 and 68) :

At the commencement of the construction of the North Devon Hallway the wages of the 'labourers were 2s. a day. During- the progress of the "work their wages Were raised to 2s. 6d. and 3s. a day. Nevertheless it -was found that the work was executed more cheaply when – the men were earning the higher rate of wage ... In carrying out a part of the Metropolitan Drainage Works in Oxford Street, the wages of the bricklayers were gradually raised from 6s. to 10s a day; yet it was found that the brickwork was constructed at a cheaper rate per cubic yard after the wages of the workmen had been raised to 10s. than when they were paid at the rate of 6s. per day

Finally, Mr. Brassey shows that, whatever the wages are, the capitalist gets his ratio of "plunder". He says (Page 75);

On my fathers extensive contracts, carded out in almost every country of the civilised world and in every quarter of the globe, the daily wage of the labourer was fixed at widely different rates; but it was found to be the almost invariable rule that the cast of labour was the same—that for. the same sum of money the same amount of work was everywhere performed.

So much for work which is performed without the aid of machinery and work that is peculiarly of a muscular character, concerning which no one could speak with greater authority.

But let it not be supposed that the efficiency even of the " manual " worker is merely a matter of food, clothing, and shelter, Mr. Edward Cadbury, in his book "Experiments in Industrial Organisation" says (pp. 3-4):

In the early days at least, half the girls taken on would be in the fifth standard, but now no girl is taken on who has not attained to the sixth standard, Within the last few years the number taken on from the seventh standard has largely increased, and on a (recent occasion, when fifty girls were taken on all were in the seventh standard, … A record was recently taken of the wages of sixth and seventh standard girls, both doing the same work under the same conditions. The results were :

At the end of three months. Sixth Standard 1.24 pence per hour. Seventh 1.33. At the end of six months, 1.58 pence per hour. 2.07 per hour.

These girls were employed at mechanical work, on piece rates, and the figures show that even in such "work the mental development is a very important factor in output.

We see, then, that the standard of subsistence of the workers may, and does, vary very widely, yet the masters have always the means, provided by the automatic development of machinery and of other ways of speeding-up, of exhausting their workers of all their productive capabilities, and, by increasing the intensity of labour as the cost of labour-power increases, of ensuring that high standards of comfort are not maintained at-the expense of profits.

Let us take it that a higher standard of subsistence and a shorter working day are possible. In theory and in practice this induces an advance of machinery. It also enables the workers to go at a higher pace, and hence encourages new methods of organisation and speeding-up. We may turn to the motor industry for an example.

In high-wage America the Ford motor plant is literally a " civil war " of production. The company's method is to pit one set of workers against another, and one worker against another. The whole plant is divided into " Production " and " Inspection "— production to obtain quantity, inspection to obtain quality. As the car moves forward on the conveyors the workers on the right-hand side are working in competition with the left, as the operations are for the most part duplicated. There is a frenzy to get an operation finished and to keep up with the conveyor, since to fall behind means holding many other workers up and risking dismissal. The " Time Records " for operations in one factory are compared with those of another. The foreman is ever bullying and driving to " get production off" and in turn is himself driven. It is necessary for him to " pitch in " and help the operations that fall behind. He must ruthlessly eliminate the slower units or be himself eliminated. He must be ever watchful to dispense with unnecessary labour. When a worker, is away from his tools for a few minutes the foreman must be ready, to take over the operation until he returns. Over all hangs the coming of the slack season, when the first to go will be the weaker units—seniority receiving no consideration. When the peak season starts again those are called in who have proved most efficient regardless of length of past service.

This, of course, was a new phase of exploitation. Years ago even the most forward employers worked on the theory that generally any five workmen taken haphazard yielded a fair average of efficiency, and little endeavour was made to select. But the higher the organisation and the more machinery is resorted to, the more is the pace of the whole retarded by the slowest operator. What this means to the weaker may be imagined. The least sign of slackness, of declining vigour, of departing youth, is doom. The six-hours' day makes possible a. pace that only the young and the strong can stand; it also calls for a severe process of elimination, and for a system of harassing and bullying hitherto unknown.

So we see that, although the standard of living of the workers varies in different countries, the higher standard by no means necessarily implies better general conditions. A higher standard of living for the working class means, from the capitalist point of view, a higher standard of efficiency and correspondingly greater possibilities of exploitation. This is why greater intensification, greater insecurity, and greater unemployment are usually found, in those countries where wages are highest.

That the struggle for higher wages and shorter hours may result in greater intensification of labour is no argument against the prosecution of that struggle. It does, however, foredoom any attempt of the workers to materially alter their conditions by means of such a struggle alone. To become tired out in six hours instead of ten may be a gain—we are not concerned to argue that it is not. The thing to be remembered is that one is tired out. The struggle, then, of itself, fails. It cannot alter the essential conditions of working-class existence. It must be maintained to resist the worsening of working-class existence, but it cannot lift the. workers from that vicious circle wherein a victory in the matter of hours or wages is answered by greater intensification of labour and increased insecurity. It can never lift them above poverty and anxiety. .

Therefore the struggle must be supplemented by something else if any extensive and permanent improvement in the position of the working class is to be secured.

Our enquiries have shown us the hopelessness of any attempt to alter the subject condition of the working class "while the present social system continues. We have seen that the reason is that every effort at such reform is defeated

by economic laws inseparable from capitalism—laws which arise from the fact that labour-power is sold. We see that labour-power can never be free from the governance of these laws while it is sold, because a sale is necessarily based upon -competition, and these economic laws are laws arising from competition, Competition springs from the desire for advantage. When the production of one class of goods is excessive, it is an economic law that the price of that class of goods falls. There is, then, less profit for the capitalists engaged in their manufacture, and again by-economic law new capital is repelled and Used in more profitable enterprises. As a consequence the output of the first class of goods is restricted, and their price recovers.

This illustration serves to show that the effects of competition are by no means accidental, but are an integral part of the competitive struggle.

What is a Social System?

There is no question, then, of abolishing these economic effects while retaining the system. Therefore, if the working class ace ever to be freed from the tyranny of economic laws which decree that they shall receive only enough to enable them to exist as an efficient labour force, with-no share in the joy of living, no business in the world but to work, it must be, not by tampering with the workings. of the social system, but by abolishing the system.

We have to deal with a social system or system of society. Let us see, then, what a system of society is.

Society is a number of persons united by certain ties, or relationships. To-day, for example, people are united by the relations of employer and employee, buyer and seller, debtor and creditor, .and so on.

These relations are called social relations.

Now the social relations do not take the same form at all times and in all places. Under the Roman Empire, for instance, the vast majority of the people of Rome were slaves Between them and their owners, therefore, there existed, not the relations of buyer and seller of labour-power, but the purely property relation which unites the horse and its owner. Like the horse, the slave was property. He did not own his labour-power, so he could not sell it, and for that reason could not enter into the same relationship with his owner as exists between the modern worker and his exploiter.

But if the social relations do not always take the same: form, they, in any given society, are always sufficiently in accord one with another to make up in the mass an orderly scheme or system. Thus the relations of buyer and seller, debtor and creditor, landlord and tenant, employer and employee, are all in accord, because they all spring from one social institution.

The sum total of these social relations, together with the instigations through which they operate, constitutes what is known as the social system, or system of society.

Every Social System has a Basis

Every social system has a definite basis or foundation on which its whole structure rests.

The basis of all settled primitive social systems, such as that of the Greeks and Romans at the dawn of history, was common, property in what was at the time the essential means of living —the land. Because every social unit had equal rights in the. soil, or, to put it more correctly, because no individual rights "in. the land existed, there were no definite class privileges. Society was, therefore, not divided into economic classes. (In order to make the position clear we have, ignored the comparatively small proportion of domestic slaves in early society.) There were no employers and workers, because the common lands afforded each the opportunity of gaining his livelihood without selling his labour-power. The social relations for this reason were those c\ social equality, and the whole structure of society, arising from and resting upon the basis of communal ownership in the means of living—the land —shaped itself, in agreement with that base, into a communistic social system.

When the people of Greece and Rome lost their communal control of the land a new social system was

developed. Society became divided into classes based on property, and the whole of the social relations changed in accordance therewith. .No longer were they relations between social equals; instead, they were relations between people rendered unequal by the new property basis of society. Those who possessed became the social superiors of those who did not possess.

It will be observed that, the reason the social system changed from primitive communism to a class society was that the social base had changed from common ownership of the means of living, in which each had an equal place, to private property in those means, which placed those who owned in a position of privilege, and reduced those who did not own to servitude.

The Basis of Modern Society

The social system prevailing to-day, like all previous systems of society, has its definite base. To this base almost every feature of modern society can be traced..

Let us take one of the main features of existing society —its division into two classes; a propertied class,, and a property less class. This is obviously, the result of the ownership of wealth of society by some of the people, to the exclusion of the others, for this alone produces a class of possessors and a class of non-possessors.

With regard to the ownership of property of all kinds, Mr. Zorn has shown (Daily News, November 29th, 1919) "that 10 per cent, of the population owns 99 per cent, of the wealth, while the remaining 1 per cent, is divided among nine-tenths of the people. And Professor Clay tells us it is probably safe to say that over two-thirds of the national capital is held by less than 2 per cent, of the people.—Times, 24th March, 1925.

The two-class -nature of the present social scheme is directly traceable to that form of private property which •excludes one class* from ownership.

As the wealth of society comprises all the means of living, its. ownership by a class .sets up that most widespread set of social relations of modern life—the relations between employer and employee. For those who do not own must become wage-workers (including the so-called salary-earners) in order to live. It is plain, therefore, that the whole institution known as the wages system arises from and rests upon the class ownership of the means of living. The relations of landlord and tenant, buyer and seller, debtor and creditor, are also ail seen to have their roots in the private property institution. Our laws are mainly property laws; our political institution is an instrument for maintaining the property system arid property interests; our marriage institution is in origin a means for legalising heirs and for establishing property relations between the parties concerned—as the. divorce court reveals in assessing monetary damages for the broken " civil contract." The very ideas current amongst us take their shape from the property basis of society, for the possessors view all things from the standpoint of property owners; and even the revolutionary idea, inasmuch as it is reaction against the present form of society, arises, finally, from that property condition —the ownership by a small section of the "community of the means and instalments for producing and distributing wealth—which, we have said, is the basis of the modern social fabric.

The Basis of the Future Social System

When we were speaking of primitive social systems we pointed out that primitive communism gave place to a class-divided social system because the basis of the social structure underwent a change. Arguing from this, it seems that we are to change the present social system by changing its basis—by substituting something else for the private ownership by a few of the people of .the means and instruments of production and distribution. We must find the substitute first.

We have seen that the present social system does not fail .in the matter of the production of wealth. Wasteful as the system is of natural resources and human energy, the fact remains that sufficient wealth is produced to. maintain every social unit in a considerable degree of comfort. To-day' some of this wealth may be of the wrong kind. We do hot want bullets for breakfast, and battleships and the like add nothing to the general comfort. But to turn bullets into water-pipes, and battleships into baths, and swords into ploughshares, is simply a matter of re-directing human energy.

The system fails in the distribution of the wealth that is produced.

We know why it fails in distribution. It is because the workers' demand upon the wealth they produce is limited to the amount which is necessary to enable them to produce it. The reason for this is, of course, that the worker has to sell his labour-power, and has only the price thereof on which to live.

This means that the new basis of society must be such as will remove from the workers the need to sell their labour-power to others. It must, therefore, give them free access to the means of living.

One thing is certain. If the workers are to have free access to the means of living, those means must not he in the ownership and control of any section of society. Either they must be divided among the whole of the people and individually owned by them, or they must be collectively owned by the whole of the people without any form of division.

The first is ruled out of court at once. We have seen that the present method of production, in spite of defects, results in ample wealth for the needs of society. This method of production could not continue if the means of production were divided among the whole of the people. A factory or a railway system directly it was divided would be useless for the purpose of producing and distributing wealth.

The fact is that the means by which man gets his living have developed beyond the stage of individual ownership "because those means have developed beyond individual operation. Only social labour—the labour of many united —can operate the modern instruments of production.

It is clear, then, that the form of ownership with which we are to replace the private ownership of today must be social ownership. Only this is in agreement with socially operated instruments of labour. If we are to retain all the advantage "which ages of evolution and invention have culminated in; if we are to reap the reward of the centuries of suffering with which the working class have paid for this perfection of productive processes, we must bring the ownership of the instruments of labour into agreement with the stage of development they have reached.

What is the difference between the Hail and the threshing

machine, the windmill and the steam flour factory, the spinning wheel and the spinning mill, the pack horse and the railway system? The most pregnant difference is that the first-named in each instance is an instrument of labour operated by one person and capable of being owned by the user, while the second in each instance is an instrument of social labour, and cannot be individually owned by those who use it If we wanted to have; individual ownership we would have to go hack to the crude implements of labour which lend themselves to such ownership. If we are to retain the gigantic means and instruments of production and distribution which make our labour so tremendously productive, we must bring the ownership of the instruments into harmony with their highly developed character.

It is because that ownership is not in harmony with the development of the means of production to-day that the workers arc in their present miserable position. The evolution of the instruments of labour has divorced their users from ownership in them. When a machine requires several people to work it they cannot all individually own and control it. But the taking of the instruments out of the possession of the workers has destroyed the sane and logical incentive of the workers to produce. The peasant proprietor., owning his own means of production, did not produce for sale, but for his own consumption. He therefore produced what he required—-bread to feed his family, clothing to cover them, and so on. But when the productive wealth ceases to belong to the user, and the latter becomes a wage worker, he cannot produce what he needs; he must produce what his employer needs. The employer needs goods to sell—it is only by selling these that he can pay his men. And above all, it is only by what is left after paying his men that the owner of the means of production himself lives.

The surplus (or rather the portion which remains after rent and interest, etc., are paid) we call profit, and it is for this profit that goods are produced to-day.

In developing the instruments of labour so that they could only be socially operated, the old incentive to produce (use) has been destroyed. No longer is bread produced to-feed the hungry, and clothing to cover nakedness, and houses to shelter those who need shelter—they are produced for profit. Hence the cry of children for bread sets no wheel of industry in motion, and people starve, not of dearth, but of glut.

Just as the means of living demand social labour to operate them, so they demand social ownership and control in order that they may be used as means of living instead of as means of producing profit. At present the workers must product more than they consume. Since, however, it is not produced to maintain them, but for sale, it heaps up in the warehouses and throws them out of work. That is because the stage of development of the instruments of labour (which has taken away from the workers the power to produce individually the things they need) and the ownership and control of those instruments, of labour, are out of harmony. They clash and conflict. In order to make them agree we must TAKE AWAY FROM THEIR PRESENT OWNERS ALL THOSE THINGS THAT ARE NECESSARY FOR THE COMFORT AND WELL-BEING OF SOCIETY AND MAKE THEM THE PROPERTY OF THE WHOLE OF SOCIETY.

That is establishing social ownership in instruments which can only be socially operated. It is enabling those who can no longer individually produce the goods they require, to produce them collectively. It will result in the social appropriation of the social products, and will, therefore, harmonise the purpose of the means of wealth production with the incentive to operate them.

The substitution, of this new property condition for the old one will abolish the existing basis of the social system and provide a new one. This is what we call the social revolution. It results in a revolution of the social structure—a complete change from, top to bottom.

Socialism

It is not for us to build up in detail the social system that will arise from the common ownership and democratic control of the instruments of labour. Our knowledge of the conditions which will prevail at the time of the change, and of the outlook upon life of people who are free to arrange matters pretty much as "they wish", is not extensive enough to warrant us seriously attempting to foretell the details of the future social system. How can we, for instance, fettered as we are by the customs and prejudices of a social system in which sexual relations are based on private property conditions, understand the views upon such matters that will obtain among women who no longer need sell their bodies for a home, and men who do .not need to fear the financial consequences of their marital acts?

We can only state the broad changes that we know must arise from the revolution in the social base.

The most obvious result of the establishment of common ownership of the means and instruments for producing and distributing wealth is. that the wages system would be abolished.

It is quite plain that there is no other course open than this. With all the means of production and distribution socially owned, no one would be in a position to exploit labour-power, therefore no one would buy it. On the other hand, with the socially owned instruments of labour open to every worker, none would wish to sell his labour-power for another s profit, even if he could find a buyer.

Thus the very conditions of wage-labour—the divorce of a portion of the community from every opportunity of gaining a livelihood save by selling their labour-power— 'having ceased to exist the whole wages system. must, perforce, tumble to the ground.

As, when the worker owned the tools he used, he produced in general only the things he required to satisfy his own needs, so society, when as a whole it owns and controls the means of-production, will produce the things society needs. Necessity alone will demand industrial activity. If warehouses then become overstocked, productive efforts will slacken; on the other hand, production will be pushed forward until all those material wants have been satisfied for which society is willing to sacrifice leisure and energy.

Another feature of the new society will be the abolition of class distinctions and privileges. To-day it is the privilege of the owners of the world's wealth that they need not perform any labour, This privilege, of course, is based on their possessions. Strip them of these and they would at once be on an equality with the other members of society. There would be nothing left for them but to work for their living like the rest.

So society would be made one. Social distinctions as we understand them to-day would no longer exist. All who were capable would be workers,- and all would draw upon the products of labour according to their needs.

Now as to appropriation. The wealth produced by social labour through socially owned instruments could only be socially owned. The individual could not own what he produced for the simple reason that no man would individually produce anything. The man who digs in a garden works with tools made by others, and approaches his ground and leaves it over roads which are the results of others' labours.

The appropriation of wealth which had been produced for no other purpose than to be used (toward the production of which all those who were physically able had contributed their share of labour) would present no difficulty. Each would freely satisfy his or her needs. The greedy scramble predicted by our opponents, who are blind enough to the "greedy" scramble for bread (at the dock gates and elsewhere) into which they force us under their system is a bogey that need frighten no one. It would only be a sign that insufficient was being produced, and the remedy would obviously be to produce more. Even the pig will turn away from the trough when it can eat no more.

These, then, are the essential features that must necessarily distinguish a social system based upon common ownership from one founded upon private property; equal opportunities for all to make the most and the best of life; social equality of all persons; production of wealth for use instead of for profit: free access for all members of the community to all the necessaries of life.

On these basic conditions, of course, men and women would shape their lives anew. Much ink has been wasted in vain forecasts of the details of that life. Some have pictured it as a "glorified barrack life," with meals taken in great dining hails, and so on. Others have drawn fanciful Arcadian pictures, ail the men supermen, all the women angels, all the children chirping cherubs with nothing to do but to look pretty and to peck here and there at hanging fruits."

Such speculations are futile, and the details in themselves are not matters of importance to us. The wishes of the majority will prevail in all matters of collective interest, and the only consideration will be the greatest happiness and welfare of the community;

52

We know that when the abolition of classes has placed every social unit on the same footing, and therefore made their interests one, the customs, manners, ethics, and ideals of humanity at large will be lifted to a higher plane.

Historical Support for Revolution

It may be asked what historical support the Socialist has for advocating a social revolution. We shall try to prove briefly that all social history supports the revolutionary idea.

It is beyond denial that the primary reason people are together in a form of society, whether they are conscious of the fact or not, is to get their living together. This is seen clearly in the simpler forms of society, such as the hunting pack. It is obvious that the primary reason for coming together was co-operation in hunting.

The methods by which the people co-operatively get their living must evidently be determined by the means at their disposal. Thus one would not expect to find top sawyers and bottom sawyers co-operating as they do until the pit-saw and the saw-pit had been invented.

If it is admitted that the methods by which people produce their living must be determined by the means by which they do so there is no escape from the revolutionary position.

The means of wealth production are always evolving. The discovery of the art of domesticating animals, of the art of agriculture, of smelting and working iron, and of the means of adapting steam as a motive force, are all epoch-making cases in point.

Now this evolution of the means of production is always more or less steadily taking place; and as the development proceeds it sets up different conditions which-make changes in the social system imperative and inevitable.

Thus the domestication of animals and the development of

agriculture made it possible for men to produce more than sufficient for their own needs, and so opened the road for a social system based upon chattel slavery—in which' slave labour produced a surplus upon which the owners of the slaves lived. The knowledge of iron and its manipulation, by affording eventually large and complicated machinery,. made possible the complete divorce of the user from ownership of the means of production, and hence produced the necessary conditions for the establishment of society based upon wage slavery—in which wage-labour produces surplus wealth upon which the owners of the means of production live.

Now the application of gas, steam and electricity to production and distribution, together with the general advance of the instruments and processes of labour, has carried society on to the point where the social base no longer suffices for the social needs, and the conditions which at one time were socially necessary have become social fetters.

Let us make our meaning plainer. It is easily under stood that, given the general conditions prevailing in the Middle Ages, the only way in which production could

develop to its present stage was through the wages system. The man who had his plot of land and operated the hand loom might own the loom, but in the development of the hand loom into the weaving factory it was necessary to make men propertyless. They were driven off the land, rendered homeless and then forced into the factory along with their families to operate for wages the factory looms that did not belong to them. At the time there was no other way in which the developing instruments of labour could be operated, therefore the divorcement of the working class from the means of production, although involving enormous suffering, worked to the ultimate advantage of the race. It enabled human labour to reach its present high state of productivity.

But the very development, the very productivity, which has resulted from the reduction of the workers from peasant-proprietors and artisans owning their own labour-instruments to wage-earners owning nothing but their labour-power, has itself rendered a change of social basis necessary. Class ownership of the means of production was essential to enable wealth to be more freely produced. It has resulted in wealth being so freely produced that class ownership has become a fetter. While the wealth which the vast bulk of the public is permitted 'to consume remains relatively stationary, the wealth which they produce increases rapidly. The surplus periodically reacts against production, and chokes it. This surplus, belonging to those who own the instruments of "labour, gluts markets and throws men out of employment. Thus the property condition that made possible such lavish wealth production, has become a drag upon the social industrial efforts.

It may be asked how it is that, if the means and methods of production evolve continuously and without violence, the social base does not also evolve smoothly and without the pain and shock of revolution.

The explanation is simple. The gradual development of the means of production forces itself on the owning class. Self-interest compels men to adopt improvements as opportunity offers. Under the present system competition forces

the owners of the machinery etc., to seek continually to render it more perfect. The only people who "might find -it to their interest to endeavour to check this development of the means of production—the working class—cannot do so because they do not control these instruments. So the means by which society gets its living develop by a process •of evolution in which the shocks of revolution do not occur.

With the social basis it is different. The social basis in private-property forms of society, has always been the result of the conscious efforts of the class which has risen to power upon it. Thus, for instance, the rising capitalist class placed society firmly on the capitalist class-ownership basis by driving the people off the land. But a class which, by revolutionary action, has succeeded in establishing that social system they desire (and which system is demanded by the stage of development of the means of production "which has brought them to power) at once ceases, to be -revolutionary. They have got the system they want, and have nothing left to revolt against. Hence from revolutionary they become reactionary, concerned only with maintaining the social basis which makes them the dominant class in society.

But if the basis of the social system remains stationary the means of production do not. These go on evolving and relentlessly undermining the position of the dominant class. They produce another revolutionary class, and press it on until it overthrows the class above, and in turn dominates -society

The basis of the power of the feudal nobility, for instance, was their control of the land in an agricultural community; but as trade and the instruments of labour developed they became superior to land as a basis for social power. These instruments of labour made the merchant capitalists richer, and this class was ultimately advanced to domination 'through the overthrow of the nobility.

The basis of the social system, then, and therefore the social system itself, while it is ultimately determined by the stage of development of the means of production, 'changes by revolution. It is changed by a victorious revolutionary class, and brought into line with the methods by which wealth is produced.

History, then, teaches us-that our emancipation must be sought in revolution.

Has the Hour Come?

What we have just- said points irresistibly to the conclusion that there is an " appointed hour " for revolution, in the sense that -it must fail if it is attempted before the general conditions are ripe. It is now our task to show that these general conditions, with the exception of that single factor, working-class knowledge, are ripe for the change.

What are the essentials that make the conditions fit and favourable for the establishment of society upon a new basis? First, the industrial processes or methods of wealth. production and distribution must have developed as far as they can under the prevailing system without injury to the social organism. Secondly, they must have reached such a stage as will allow the revolutionary class to assume control of them and operate them.

That the first condition has been reached is shown by the spread of capitalism over the earth: It is a characteristic of the present system of production that ever-increasing markets at home or abroad must be found to absorb the growing volume of surplus products which its wage-earners produce.

There remain now no considerable tracts of country to be thrown open to commerce. On the other hand, nations which until lately had been the safety-valves of the great manufacturing countries, are now fast becoming the competitors of these latter. There is no Dominion of any importance that has not industrial aspirations. When, for example, the Canadians proposed to furnish ships for the " Empire's" navy, they were to be Canadian built. Russia is on the way to becoming an Important competitor in the world market. The entry of Japan into capitalist manufacture is an old story, but the case of Turkey,. Persia, and other Eastern countries is a tale of. to-day. When, some years ago, an East London jute factory closed down, and hundreds of girls were thrown into the-streets, the explanation of the owner was that he could not continue in the face of foreign competition. The " foreign competition " was a factory established by the London jute manufacturer in India!

Indianow has an industrial population at least equal to that of France, and greater than that of either Italy or Japan.

But the crowning act is the capture by capitalism of the mighty Chinese Empire. The conversion of the immense, and densely populated quarter of the globe from a feudal monarchy into a capitalist republic shows what power capitalism has attained in the flowery land.

As these newer capitalist countries develop their manufacturing powers, and more and more compete in the world market, the industrial crises and periods of stagnation caused by " over-production " and- congested markets, must force the workers ultimately to seek a solution for the problem.

The mad pitch to which production is being screwed up to-day is producing disastrous results upon the race. The physical deterioration which is taking place among the most advanced capitalist nations is a source of anxiety to those who are hard put to it to find men equalling the original standard set for the bearing of arms, while the steady but striking increase 'of lunacy and suicides is eloquent of the danger humanity is in from further development along present lines.

The development of the means of production has also made it possible for the working class to carry on all productive operations for themselves by the simple process of removing the master class from production and distribution and leaving the workers to it. The joint stock company is the type of the exploiting organisation to-day The vast bulk of the world's capital is owned by these concerns.

This form of organisation effectually separates the owners from all connection with wealth production. The shareholder cannot even pretend that he takes any part in it. He has not even, legally, any right to set foot in the factory in whose possession he shares. He may not, and probably does not, know where and how the profit is produced which his shares bring him. The board of directors 'which' the shareholders elect are not appointed even to supervise production, but only' to secure the profits. All the necessary work of production and distribution, the organisation no less than the operation, is performed by members of the working class—by men and women who, however high their position or their pay, have to sell their "labour-power for wages or salary in order to live.

Thus it is seen that the development of industry has rendered the capitalist class quite superfluous. Whatever useful function they may at one time have fulfilled, there is in typical cases, no shred of it left to-day.- We know, then, that the working class can .carry on the work, of the world without the assistance of the capitalists because they are practically doing so already. They have become the only useful class in society, and-for this reason the thing that is needed to make the conditions ripe for the establishment of Socialism is adequate economic and political knowledge on the part of the working class.

By what means the revolutionary working class are to proceed to their task of overthrowing the present social system and establishing a system of society based upon the common ownership of the means of living, is the next question that demands our attention. It is a question of vital importance.

– The means by which the ruling class maintain their social system and their dominance long after it ceases to meet the requirements of society are mainly coercive. The police, military, naval and air forces—the armed forces of the State— are the chief bulwark by which they protect their social edifice against the assaults of those who would-overthrow it.

It needs very little thought to convince one that it would be the height of folly to expect or to attempt to dispossess the possessing class so long as they have under their control such mighty forces of repression as these. What the result would be is indicated by many tragic episodes, both of home and abroad, from the ferocious suppression of the Commune of Paris in 1871 (when the master class of France, with the approval of the master class of the whole world, butchered over 30,000 working men-, women and children after resistance had ceased), to the crushing of revolts In Austria, Spain arid elsewhere in the present century.

The workers must therefore, as the first essential, step in the dethroning of the capitalist class, gain control; of the armed forces of the State.

These armed forces are controlled by the House of Commons. There is voted the money that supports them. There is decided whether they shall be extended or reduced, whether they shall be voluntary or compulsory, and in the ultimate, whether they shall be launched against any object of capitalist fear, greed or. malice.

The course the workers have to follow, then, is plain to view. They must capture the political machinery through which the

armed forces and other means of repression are controlled-
Parliament, where the naval and military forces are controlled
and the laws made; the local councils and governing bodies,
which administer the laws and control the " civil" forces.

This political machinery must be captured by the workers
organising themselves into a political party, having for its
object the overthrow of the present social system and the
establishment of a system of society based upon common
ownership of the means of living. Thus organised they must
wrest control of the political machinery from the ruling class
by means of the ballot, and having achieved this control, must
use it to strip the capitalist class of their possessions, and
consequently of their privileges.

The vote is to be the weapon. Let us inquire, therefore, what is
the real nature of the vote.

At one time men supported their interests by force, of arms.
Gradually it was recognised that, other things being equal,
power, rests with numbers. From this to the idea that those-who
possess militant power can express it just-as effectually and
much more conveniently by a vote than by a blow, is but a step.
Thus we find the vote in existence ; at the very dawn of
authentic history.

A vote, it is thus seen, is "something more than a cross on a
scrap of paper. In this respect it is very similar to a bank-note.
A bank-note of itself is practically valueless. It derives its
"bank-note value" entirely from the public confidence in the
security at the back of it. Where any doubt exists as to this the
fact is indicated in the depreciation of the "value" of the paper
money. Exactly so with the vote. No section of society obtains
voting power until it proves by struggle that its demands cannot
be ignored. It then becomes to the advantage of the dominant

-class to permit these demands to be expressed through the ballot rather than through the disruptive and wasteful channel of open struggle.

The value of the vote is measured by the man behind the vote.

That being so, then, it is clear that it is not the elected representative who is the all-important factor, but the quality of the vote which puts him into place.

What, then must be the quality of the vote? Surely the quality that will enable it to effect its purpose. The revolutionary purpose being revolution, the votes cast for the revolutionary representative must be revolutionary votes. They must be the votes of those who understand the need for revolution, desire it, and are determined to achieve it.

What are the respective positions of men returned to Parliament or other elected public bodies by votes of this quality and those elected by votes of the politically uninformed who do not clearly understand what it is they want?

The former is the servant of his constituents. Understanding the position, they are able to direct his course of action, hence they are his masters. If he plays them false, if he departs from the revolutionary path, they know it at once, and seize the first opportunity of "dealing with him. On the other hand, such a representative knows that in all sound revolutionary action he has the full support of those whose delegate he is, and hence becomes the strong and efficient servant of a strong master.

The representative of the politically uninformed is in an entirely different position. As he gets his votes on all manner of vague pretexts and promises, the only safe course, for him is a vague wobble. A definite course in any direction would result in the alienation of support. He therefore dares not attempt to take a revolutionary course, whatever his views may be, for he has all sorts and conditions of persons in his following except revolutionists— the revolutionist does not follow.

Such a representative is in a position to sell his electors.. Depending upon confusion for his place, his best chance of maintaining it is to preserve that confusion. This suits the capitalists very well, for their chief concern is that the workers shall not know who their enemies are.. Therefore, the political parties of the capitalist class welcome such representatives of Labour—they know there is no revolutionary force behind them.

The first essential, then, of having a vote of revolutionary quality is to have a working class that thoroughly -understands its position in society, that thoroughly realises' the hopelessness of any endeavour to improve materially that position under the present social scheme, and that therefore is thoroughly resolved to abolish the system and establish Socialism; the crying need, then, is knowledge.

The first thing that the workers must learn is that there is only one working class, and that their interests are one and the same the wide world over. Then they must learn that, just as the workers are made one by common interest, so a common interest; binds the capitalists of the world into a solid class. The realisation of this teaches the lesson that the interests of the workers and the capitalists are diametrically opposed, for this follows from the fact that it is interests that divide the people into classes. The logical implication of this is that the workers must proceed to work out their emancipation as a class. This means organisation-—the closest, .the highest, most perfect organisation possible—organisation on class lines.

The Essentials of the Political Organisation

The political organisation of the working class, having for its object the establishment of the Socialist system by a politically educated working class, must first of all be" an instrument capable of fulfilling its purpose. It must, then, be firmly anchored to its object so that it is impossible for it to drift. The first thing needed, therefore, is a clear statement of what the object is. It must be clear because the party seeking working-class emancipation can only gain its object through men and women who thoroughly understand what that object is. Those who hold that it is the 'leader" or "representative who is the source of power are" of course, quite logical in adopting an " object" that will appeal to the greatest numbers.. In such a case all that is wanted is shoulders to climb upon. The ' leaders " being the strength of the organisation, it is quite sufficient' that they understand the object of the organisation—the others do not matter.

The case is very different with a democratic organisation. The first principle of such is that it is the workers as a class who must fight the battle for emancipation; it is they who must be strong, since their servants and delegates can be strong only with their strength. The logic of this is that the fitness of the organisation for its purpose depends upon the quality and strength, not of ' leaders," but of the membership. .

The first essential, then, of the political party of the . working class is a clear and definitely stated Object. The statement of Object of the Socialist Party of Great Britain is a clear and definite statement of the Socialist object, ft hides nothing, and contains the most correct and concise definition of Socialism that has yet been formulated. It is:

The establishment of a system of society based upon the common ownership and democratic control of the means and instruments for producing and distributing wealth by and in the interest of the whole community.

In this Object there is nothing but the revolutionary purpose. There are no side issues to cause "dissension and to sap the working-class movement of its vitality.

The next essential is to anchor the party to that Object. For this purpose it is necessary to lay down a definite set of principles, based upon the facts of the working-class position, and indicating the path to be followed in pursuit of the party's Object, and the test for all its members' actions.

The S. P. G. B. declares in the first clause of the declaration of Principles:

"That society as at present constituted is based upon the ownership of the means of living (i.e., land, factories, railways, etc.) by the capitalist or master class, and the consequent enslavement of the working class by whose labour alone wealth is produced."

We have sufficiently proved, by what we have said in the foregoing pages, that the basis of society is the class ownership of the means of living, and that this results in the non-possessors having to sell themselves for wages— to become wage-slaves—and to produce not only the wealth they consume,, but also the wealth consumed by the possessing class. . The second clause is:

That in society, therefore, there is an antagonism of interests, manifesting itself as a class struggle, between those who possess but do not produce, and those who produce but do not possess. This is really a deduction from the first. Since society is divided into two classes, one of which is enslaved to the other, one of which exploits, preys, upon the other/ there must necessarily be an antagonism of interest. The interest of one class is to maintain its position of dominance; the interest of the other class is to escape from its position of servitude. Any lifting or sinking of individuals from one class to another does not affect this position. The masters can only maintain their position as a class; the workers can only achieve their emancipation as a class. Clearly, then, the interests, being class interests, must result in a class struggle—a struggle between those who possess, to maintain the private property basis of society1 that makes them masters of the world, and those who do not possess to abolish the property condition that reduces them to servitude.

The third clause is as follows:

"That this antagonism can be abolished only by the emancipation of the working class from the domination of the master class, by the conversion into the common property of society of the means of production and distribution, and their democratic control by the whole people."

Those who want office, who are " determined to get our feet on the floor of the House of Commons and are not particular how we do it" (because that is all they want), claim that the emancipation of the working class does not need a revolution. The reason for this is easily seen.. The only way in which they could get their feet on the floor of the House of Commons to-day is by denying the need for revolution.

Revolution and the class struggle of course are necessarily

connected. The "gradualist," therefore, in order that he may get his feet on the floor of the House of Commons with the help of non-socialist votes, is forced to deny the revolution because that implies recognising the existence of the class struggle.

Those, however, who realise the facts of the political situation, know that the workers would not be driven to seek emancipation but for the class antagonism; hence they are driven to accept the class struggle as the very basis of their action. So the seventh clause declares for war upon class lines in the following words:

That as political parties are but the expression of class interests, and as the interest of the working class is diametrically opposed to the interests of all sections of the master class, the party seeking working-class emancipation must he hostile to every other party.

There is the sheet anchor of the revolutionary party. It is this which, beyond all else, secures to the consciously organised working class the efficiency of their organisation for its revolutionary purpose. While adherence to this vital principle remains one of the conditions of membership of the Socialist Party, it can never become the plaything of leaders and dictators. A membership holding to that clause has a gauge wherewith to measure any man's action, and an instrument to fire him out with, if he be found wanting. The first sign of-compromise, the first-indication. of alliance with the enemy, the first particle of evidence that a member has become the tool of any section of the master class, and he is dealt with by a membership imbued with the principle of the class struggle.

Based upon such principles as these, the political party of the working class cannot drift away from its Object, and must remain a sound, organisation, an instrument capable of

achieving its purpose. Just as it can only be composed of
Socialists, of men and women conscious of their class position
and the remedy for it—the men and women who alone are
capable of achieving the Social Revolution—so it is capable of
creating such a class-conscious working class, by its clear-cut,
class struggle, revolutionary policy. This policy leaves no
doubt as to the-enemy, it leaves no doubt as to the character of
the struggle that dictates it. And, above all, it leaves no doubt
as to the strength of the revolutionary movement.

For when every vote is asked for in opposition to Liberal and
Tory, in opposition to I.L.P., Labour Party, and Communists, in
opposition to reformist confusion and vote-catching slogans—
asked for (to use the words of the sixth clause of our.
Declaration of Principles) " For the conquest of the powers of
government," every vote will be found a sound vote—a vote
which owes the master class nothing, and from which they can
take nothing away —a vote backed by the revolutionary force
of the voter, and therefore a vote to strike fear into the hearts of
our exploiters.

In concluding our case, we desire to emphasise again the most
important facts. The first is that terrible poverty exists among
the workers to-day. The second is that though the command of
man over nature, and the productivity of human labour, have
increased enormously during the last 500 years, the bulk of the
workers, in view of the vastly increased production of wealth,
are poorer to-day than they were in the Middle Ages. The third
is that this poverty is worst when the warehouses and grain
elevators are full to bursting and the markets glutted. The
fourth is sufficient wealth is produced to-day to afford
comparative comfort to every member of the community. The
fifth is that the work of producing and distributing that wealth
is performed by the working class. The sixth is that this work is

performed by men and women who together, probably, would not number more than half the male population between the ages of 16 and 60.

Are these six statements true? If they are, then all that is required; is that working-class. intelligence, courage, and determination shall rise to the height of seizing "this sorry scheme of things entire," and remoulding it to the end that the general happiness and well-being shall be the sole purpose of all productive effort. If they are true they impose upon every working man and woman the serious duty of giving thought to these matters; for it is from them alone that the remedy can come. The salvation of the working class involves the overthrow of the master class, therefore it is futile to look for help from the latter.

Fellow-workers, the evolutionary process -which has brought the workers to slavery has brought us now the opportunity of freedom.' It has' done more also. In bringing the means of living to that stage of development where they may be the instrument of the' workers' emancipation, just as they were, long ages ago, the instrument of their enslavement, it has given us means of living which can only remain means of living in the hands of a free people.

1It is true that there are articles which sell permanently above their value or permanently below, but this does not affect the above argument, because it is still value that is the determining factor in fixing the point about which price fluctuates.

• Further reading – Socialist Classics

Unit 1 – Short introductory works

1. The Communist Manifesto (1848) Karl Marx and Friedrich Engels

2. Wage-labour and capital (1847) Karl Marx

3. Value, Price and Profit (1865) Karl Marx

4. Socialism: Utopian and Scientific (1880) Friedrich Engels

5. The German Ideology (1846) Karl Marx and Friedrich Engels

6. Anarchism and Socialism (1895) Georgi Plekhanov

7. No Compromise, No Political Trading (1899) Wilhelm Liebknecht

8. Reform or Revolution (1900) Rosa Luxemburg

9. Leninism or Marxism? (1904) Rosa Luxemburg

10. Socialism Made Easy (1909) James Connolly